DUTCH

OVEN

COOKING

DUTCH OVEN COOKING

Fourth Edition

John G. Ragsdale

ILLUSTRATED BY G. F. ZINKGRAF

TAYLOR TRADE PUBLISHING

Lanham ~ New York ~ Boulder ~ Toronto ~ Oxford

Published by Taylor Trade Publishing
An imprint of
The Rowman & Littlefield Publishing Group, Inc.
4501 Forbes Boulevard, Suite 200, Lanham, Maryland 20706

Distributed by NATIONAL BOOK NETWORK

Library of Congress Cataloging-in-Publication Data
Ragsdale, John G.
    Dutch oven cooking / John G. Ragsdale. — 4th ed.
        p.   cm.
    Includes index.
    ISBN-13: 978-1-58979-352-1 (pbk. : alk. paper)
    ISBN-10: 1-58979-352-8 (pbk. : alk. paper)
    1. Outdoor cookery. 2. Dutch oven cookery. I. Title.
    TX823.R24 2006
    641.5'89—dc22   2005035589

Manufactured in the United States of America.

CONTENTS

THE OVEN   1

COOKING HELPS   17

MEATS, FISH & EGGS   23

VEGETABLES & SOUPS   39

DESSERTS   55

BREADS 77

SOURDOUGH 87

ACKNOWLEDGMENTS

I want to recognize the valuable support from my wife, De De, for her continuing review of recipes; from all of my children for tolerance and suggestions; and from the many other persons who contributed recipes, ideas, and cooking practices.

PREFACE

*T*his book is intended to provide a source of good meals for anyone who is planning the menu or will be cooking the meals for a group of six to eight, or for anyone interested in preparing good meals in camp. It is not intended for the complete use of the culinary manager or the advanced degree of a gourmet cook.

The book is bound in a size that can be carried easily in your camp gear. Your favorite recipes added to this book will enlarge its usefulness; therefore, you may write in your own recipes in the blank areas at the end of the chapters and index.

Each item is included so that it might contribute to your enjoyment of camping and cooking outdoors. I hope this volume encourages the hesitant, helps the inexperienced, challenges the interested, and increases the pleasure of those who enjoy Dutch oven cooking.

THE OVEN

HISTORY OF THE DUTCH OVEN

Many articles have been written about the origin, development, and use of the Dutch oven in past years, and these provide many interesting moments of reading. For our purpose, we want to recognize that the Dutch oven came to this country in its early years of development, and it was an item of great use in preparing pleasant, nourishing meals for thousands of people. As settlers moved across our land, this cooking utensil was probably the most important one on the wagon or pack animal.

Through the years, many hunters, fishermen, ranchers, trappers, Scouts and campers of all styles have found the Dutch oven a most useful utensil. Probably your most versatile cooking tool, it can be used for frying, browning, steaming, stewing and baking. Most anything that can be cooked in or on your kitchen stove at home can be cooked in the Dutch oven in your camp.

CHOOSING YOUR DUTCH OVEN

I hope choosing your Dutch oven will be the first step in a long series of interesting and pleasant times on your camping ventures.

A good source is the local Boy Scouts of America equipment distributor who will have a stock of Dutch ovens or can readily obtain one from his supply source. Many of the better sporting goods stores will be a source for buying an oven.

The size of ovens may range from 8 inches to about 16 inches in diameter, but the most common size is 12 inches in diameter and is the size I would suggest for your purchase. This size is usually ample for use in serving six to eight persons, is a satisfactory size for storing and transporting on your outings, and is most readily available.

You may choose an oven that is either cast iron or aluminum, each material providing some advantages. The 12-inch aluminum type weighs only seven pounds and, by nature of the metal, is not susceptible to rusting. The 12-inch aluminum oven also reflects heat very well and consequently requires more coals than the cast iron oven to provide the same degree of heat inside the oven. You may notice the heat variation in times of high wind or low temperatures. For backpacking, canoeing trips or weight problems, this may be your best choice.

The cast iron oven is heavier—weighing 18 pounds—and will rust unless it is properly oiled in usage and storage. This type of oven, however, retains heat very well and provides a more constant, even temperature. I have used a cast iron oven for a number of years and prefer it, although I enjoy the aluminum ovens too.

The best oven for your use will have three legs, which will serve to keep the oven above the ground at a sufficient height to allow placing coals under the bottom of the oven. These legs are essential for the best use of the oven, and you should use care not to break them in handling the oven. Do not make the mistake of choosing a flat bottom, indoor type of oven that works well in your kitchen, but is not the type for your outdoor cooking.

There are some ovens made with a long handle on the side to allow the oven to be placed in a deep cooking recess or to be lifted more comfortably from a hot fire. I find that this type is more difficult to store and carry. The long handle is also clumsy in a small fire area. For these reasons, I cannot recommend this style for your purchase.

Also, the best ovens have a vertical lip around the edge of the lid, and this lip is more important in retaining coals on the top of your oven. This lip also can serve as a place to grasp to remove the lid during cooking, The rounded, self-basting top works well in your kitchen at home but is not the type you need on your camping trip.

Another item to look for when purchasing an oven is the closed (looped) handle on the top center of the lid, which allows for lifting the lid during cooking. When the top is covered with coals, you can hook the handle with a lifter to remove the lid.

A heavy wire bail should be connected to two ears on the sides of the oven. This bail is useful in rotating or moving the oven when cooking is in progress and, of course, is used to carry the cool oven in the usual loading and transportation. You will discover the value of this bail when lifting the hot oven during cooking.

Using Your Dutch Oven

Preparation

The first matter to accomplish with your cast iron oven is to season it properly. This and subsequent care for your oven will be valuable to you in using and learning to appreciate your oven.

When the oven was shipped from the manufacturer, it may have been coated with a waxy layer of material to protect it until you receive it. First, remove this material by a gentle washing in warm, sudsy water to allow the bare metal to be exposed. Next, rinse the oven and allow it to dry by placing it in a warm, open area.

Your next step is to coat the oven and lid with a thin layer of oil, allowing this oil to seal or fill the metal pores. For this and subsequent coatings of the oven, you should use a salt-free shortening or, if you must, oleomargarine or butter; if none of these are available, you can use some suet or meat grease or some edible oil to protect the metal from dust or moisture.

After the oven is coated, rub a small amount of shortening in the oven and heat at a moderate temperature for an hour. This may be done on an open fire or in your home oven. After cooking, wipe the oven, leaving a thin layer of shortening on all the metal surfaces. Every time you remove the oven from the heat, leave the lid ajar so that moisture will not condense inside the oven. Your oven will form a patina, or finish, with continued usage. This seasoned surface is evidence of use and care of the oven.

When you are ready to use your oven each time, examine the oven to be sure the oil coating is still well spread over all the metal. I like to rewipe the oven each time to be sure to remove any dust or foreign particles which may have fallen into the oven, and also to confirm a coating on the metal.

This same attention is not required for your aluminum oven, since it does not rust with exposure to moisture. However, I do give it the same careful treatment of cleaning so that it will be ready for service at the next campfire.

Tools

I find that one good tool to use in lifting the lid by the center handle is a double wire lifter. The wire can be $1/16$-inch gauge wire or some other available piece of wire. Cut a length of wire about 24 inches long and bend it double, allowing a space of about 2 inches between the two parallel sides of the wire. Next, bend a small hook on the bottom inch of each cut end of the wire. This gives you a double length of wire to hook under the lid handle, and the 2-inch space allows a place to put a finger or two to assure good control in lifting the lid. You may want to make the handle slightly longer to give you some additional space between the knuckles and the coals on the lid—experience will dictate.

The lifter can also be used as tongs or forceps to lift small charcoal pieces or briquets for your oven. This lifter is an inexpensive and useful tool that can be easily replaced. Of course, any long handled tongs that can be used to lift and move coals to your oven will be helpful, if it is convenient for you to bring them with your camp equipment.

Some lid lifters are available with a double hook. This balances the lid when lifting, which keeps the coals from spilling from the lid. A balanced lid prevents ashes and coals from falling into food that is cooking in your oven.

The hot pot tongs sold by the Dutch oven distributor are also recommended for use with your oven and with other utensils at your fire. These tongs can be used to lift the oven lid by the top handle or by the lip. A hook on the tongs is also useful in handling the bail if it is too hot for your hand.

Another helpful tool to have is a shovel. The shovel can stir wood in the fire for better burning and can be used to lift coals from the fire to the oven. The handle length can provide a more comfortable method of removing coals from the fire for your oven.

The lid on your oven should have a tight fit when in place; this will provide a pressure seal to keep the oven at optimum heat for your cooking. When the lid is placed on the oven, a slight rotation of the lid will assist in better sealing if any grit or particle is present on the edge of the lid or oven. Be careful not to damage the seal area of either the lid or oven body when using or transporting the oven.

Many cooks find that leather gloves are desirable for camp cooking. The gloves provide a shield to keep reflected heat off your hands, but

this is for a limited time, beyond which the leather may actually retain enough heat to steam your hands. Gloves may serve as hot mitts for lifting lids or tools, but only for a short time. Carry a thick hot mitt or pad for such a purpose. The gloves will also help keep soot off your hands. Generally, I prefer the tools rather than the gloves.

Lid

Inverting the lid will provide an excellent griddle for cooking eggs, pancakes, or French toast. Although the lid will have a slight impression in the center, it will not prove unmanageable. Adequate oiling of the lid will prevent sticking during this cooking.

Coals

Coals for your oven can be natural coals from a wood fire, prepared lump charcoal, or briquets. Use of natural wood coals means that you do not have to carry charcoal with you, but you must have wood available for a fire. The best wood for charcoal forming is hardwood such as oak or hickory, which will provide firm, continuously burning coals.

Lump charcoal can be carried as a supplemental fuel and can be ignited in the fire, then placed on the oven. Use of briquets is even

STEP 3.

← BRIQUETS

← PAPER

STEP 4.

more convenient and efficient. The briquets can be ignited in the fire or in a separate container and subsequently used for your oven. These briquets provide a concentrated heat and will burn continuously. If you camp in areas where dead wood is in short supply, carry charcoal as a routine, helpful supplement.

A convenient charcoal briquet igniter is a gallon can with holes punched along the bottom edge of the can's side. A drink can opener does an excellent job, and holes spaced closely together provide adequate air for the fire. Take a double sheet of newspaper and gently stuff it into the bottom one-third of the can. Add enough briquets to fill another one-third of the can. Ignite the paper and allow the fire to burn the paper and subsequently ignite the briquets. A small breeze or air flow will ensure proper burning of the paper and charcoal; if there is no breeze, you may need to fan the can to force air into the fire space in the bottom of the can.

Once you have the briquets ignited, you may place more briquets in the can for ignition. Stirring the contents of the can now will place the new briquets in among the burning ones and will provide earlier ignition of all of the briquets. I have done this, sometimes repeatedly removing burning briquets and placing in new ones, thereby having a continuous source of briquets for use. This works very well when you have several Dutch ovens going for one meal.

The amount of charcoal needed for your oven will vary because of the type of coals, type of food being prepared, amount of wind, temperature and altitude. But you will learn to compensate for these differences by continued experience and by observation of your food cooking.

You will find that the briquets give more concentrated heat than natural coals do. A strong wind will also cause the coals to burn faster and provide a hotter oven than they will on a still, breezeless day. Of course, you can imagine that an oven on a 100° summer day will probably need fewer coals than the same food in the same oven on a 20° day. Also, the perennial problem of altitude must be remembered—more coals will be required as the altitude increases.

Baking

Prior to using the oven for any type of cooking, it should be preheated. This consists of nothing more than placing some coals under and on top of the oven a few minutes before cooking. This makes your oven near or at the necessary temperature when you are ready to add the food. This also will aid in preventing the food from sticking to the oven.

Baking will usually require a few coals under the oven with most of the coals on top of the oven. A general rule is to have about one-third of the coals below and two-thirds on top. Having too many on the bottom may overcook the baking food. More coals on top give high heat to the baking air space in the oven and then directly down to your food. I find that for a 12" oven about 7 to 8 charcoal briquets underneath and 15 to 18 on top give good baking heat.

When baking cookies or pies in a flat pie pan or when cooking a casserole dish in the oven, it is good to have the dish slightly elevated to avoid overheating the bottom of the container. I often place three metal washers or two metal tent pins on the bottom of the oven to support a pan and allow heated oven air to circulate under it. Any metal piece should be unplated so that it will not shed a coating or melt.

Sometimes you may want to drop biscuit or cookie dough from a spoon directly onto the bottom of the oven. Be certain that the oven is well-greased. Also, the temperature of the bottom of the oven should be reduced to prevent overcooking the food; this can be done by removing some of the coals from under the oven.

When cooking muffins, you will not have a round pan with muffin spaces, so you must prepare otherwise. Some cooks use cupcake papers that are prepared with an outer layer of aluminum foil. This type of cupcake holder is convenient, but often the weight of the batter overloads and flattens the papers, causing the batter to spill. Also, the foil wrappers are not fully disposable in your cleanup fire.

My favorite method for baking muffins is to place the cupcake papers in individual aluminum dessert molds for firm support. When the batter is poured in the cupcake papers, the sides are fully supported throughout cooking. When the muffins are done, invert the aluminum molds, and the paper-wrapped muffins are ready to serve. The paper wrapper is fully disposable in the fire; the aluminum mold is clean, ready for storage; and the inside of your oven is clean, ready for inspection and cooling.

Other Cooking

For boiling, deep frying, and stewing, you will want more coals or briquets on bottom where this higher heat will be transmitted to the liquid in the oven and then on to your food. You may want to make your coal ratio two-thirds below and one-third on top, since heat from the bottom is the most important heat. Those dishes with liquid in the oven usually cook best with small bubbles breaking through the liquid at a steady pace.

When recipes call for browning the ingredients, you should have coals below the oven and have the lid off. This will allow the ingredients to quickly seal over and brown on the outside. For deep-fat frying or some boiling, you will also want the lid removed. For baking, you will always want the lid in place and covered with coals because these coals are the source of the high, dry heat that surrounds the food and provides the baking delights of the oven.

Since there are many premeasured dry mixes on the market, there are dozens of cakes, cookies, pies, and breads that you can readily prepare and serve hot from your oven. This will allow you to supplement the wonderful breads and desserts that you can prepare from scratch. The current canned, dehydrated, dried, and frozen meats and vegetables also give you untold numbers of nourishing, tasty foods that can come from your oven.

Stacking

One additional idea is to use several Dutch ovens and stack them vertically. The basic advantage of this is that the coals on top of the lower oven will also provide heat to the bottom of the upper oven. Two or three ovens may be stacked in this manner. One disadvantage of this oven-stacking method is that the stack must be removed any time you want to inspect food in a lower oven. Also, the amount of coals on top of one oven may provide a different amount of heat from that which is needed for the food in the oven above. I prefer to use several ovens separately, but you may find this stacking useful on some occasions.

CLEANING YOUR DUTCH OVEN

If you bake cookies, pies, breads or casseroles in containers in the oven, the "cleaning the oven" step is eliminated. Rechecking the oven for a protective oiled film will be all that is necessary when the oven cools.

Many times, after cooking biscuits or some dry dough item directly on the bottom of the oven, you can wipe the crumbs from the oven and do no further cleaning, except rechecking the oven for a protective oiled film on the metal.

After a greasy or sugary meal has been cooked directly in the oven, you must clean it. Do not use soap inside the oven, since soap particles may seep into the pores of the metal and be forced out again at the next oven use. These particles might affect the flavor and purity of your next meal. The best way to clean the messy oven is to put hot water into the oven and replace it on the fire, bringing the water almost to a boil. Remember, add only hot water to a heated oven because a great temperature difference might cause the oven metal to crack. Then, using a soft scrubber, such as plastic mesh, gently scrub the remaining food from the oven sides and bottom, discarding the cleaning fluid. You may repeat this cleaning, if needed. Do not use a metal scrubber or steel wool, since this will scratch or remove the patina from your oven.

After the oven is clean, place it near the fire so that it will heat dry, removing any moisture from the metal. When the oven is dry, remove it to cool. After the oven is cool enough to handle, apply a coating of shortening to the metal to again provide a protective coating to the metal. To apply the shortening, you can use a pastry brush, paper towel, scrap of cotton cloth, or even your fingers.

I usually apply shortening only to the inside of the oven, since that is what usually has been wet and needs the oiled protection. If you detect any rusting on the outside of the oven or if it has been exposed to outside moisture or rain, you may want to apply shortening to the outside metal surface. I prefer not to oil my aluminum ovens after cleaning, since they do not require a protective oil coating. Check your oven after each use to give it the best protection and make it ready for the best service next time.

Remember to remove the lid or slide it ajar when you remove the oven from the heat. Also remember to store the lid ajar or with a stick or some other object between the lid and oven so that air may circulate in the oven and minimize moisture inside. Your oven should always be air-cooled. Never cool it with water because overrapid cooling can cause warping or cracking.

Pie Pan Dutch Oven

Another idea for Dutch oven cooks is to construct and use a pie pan oven. This oven is composed of three pie pans—the bottom one in the regular position for containing the food to be cooked; the middle one inverted over the first pan as a lid for the oven; and the top pan in regular position to hold the top coals. The middle pan and the top pan must be bolted together so that when you lift the upper pan of coals, you will also lift the middle pan lid. This allows removal of the top section with one hand when you want to inspect or move the food in the oven. These two pans can be bolted with one bolt and wing nut placed in a hole made in the center of both pans. A more secure method is to use two bolts and nuts in two holes about 3 to 4 inches apart in the central portion of both pans. Two bolts and nuts also give you a safety factor. In case you lose one nut or bolt, you still have one set to use until a replacement can be secured. In cooking, these holes will be used to join the middle and upper pans as one piece. In storage, the bolt or bolts can be removed; the two pans can be turned to nest together, and the bolt or bolts can be replaced in the holes to keep pans, bolts and nuts together in a more compact space. Then, the third pan can be nested with the other two for storage.

For best results, use heavy gauge, 9-inch aluminum pie pans. Lightweight, alloy pans rust, warp, and don't conduct heat efficiently. Use bolts and wing nuts made of a material that will not melt or shed a coating when heated. I use brass ones and have had good results. I have also seen some steel ones that give satisfactory service.

Your bottom pan must be elevated a bit above the ground so that coals can be placed under the oven. I have used rocks, but my preference is to use three metal tent stakes equally spaced about two-thirds of the distance from the center of the oven. These stakes can be lowered or raised to provide the correct distance above your coals, probably about 2 inches.

Since aluminum is such a good reflector of heat, I have tried to retain more heat in the oven by painting all surfaces except the two inside food surfaces with black boiler paint. I have cooked in identical ovens with and without the black paint coating, and it seems that there is an improvement with the paint. I cannot provide scientific proof, but any small assistance is help in your favor.

A pie pan oven is excellent for a backpacking or canoeing trip when you need minimum space and weight requirements. It also is a good supplemental oven on any trip for baking biscuits or corn bread when another portion of your meal is cooking in your regular Dutch oven. My aluminum pie pan oven and aluminum hot pot tongs are standard packing items.

COOKING HELPS

Useful Accessories

- Measuring spoons: 1 tbsp, 1 tsp, $^1/_2$ tsp, $^1/_4$ tsp
- Measuring cup with division marks for each $^1/_4$ cup volume
- Long-handled spoon
- Long-handled fork
- Long-handled tongs
- Short-handled spatula
- Hot pot tongs
- Small shovel
- Lid lifter
- Shortening
- Individual aluminum dessert molds
- Cupcake papers

MEASUREMENTS

3 teaspoons = 1 tablespoon
4 tablespoons = $^1/_4$ cup = 2 ounces
5 $^1/_3$ tablespoons = $^1/_3$ cup
1 cup = 8 ounces = $^1/_2$ pint
2 cups = 16 ounces = 1 pint
4 cups = 1 quart
$^1/_3$ cup dry milk plus $^7/_8$ cup water = 1 cup milk
1 $^1/_3$ cups dry milk plus 3 $^3/_4$ cups water = 4 cups milk = 1 quart
1 stick butter = $^1/_4$ pound = $^1/_2$ cup = 8 tablespoons

EMERGENCY SUBSTITUTIONS

1 cup milk = $^1/_2$ cup evaporated milk plus $^1/_2$ cup water
1 cup buttermilk = 1 tablespoon vinegar plus enough sweet milk
to make 1 cup
1 tablespoon cornstarch = 2 tablespoons flour
1 cup butter = 1 cup cooking oil

ABBREVIATIONS AND METRIC CONVERSION

oz = ounce	1 pint = 471 ml
1 tsp = 5 ml	pkg = package
tsp = teaspoon	1 qt = 942 ml
1 tbsp = 15 ml	qt = quart
tbsp = tablespoon	1 oz = 28 grams
1 cup = 237 ml	ml = milliliter
lb = pound	1 lb = 454 grams

HINTS

• Instead of butter, you may substitute oleomargarine or shortening.
• Test cakes and muffins for doneness by sticking a toothpick, pin, or straw into the middle of the item. If no batter sticks to it when it is withdrawn, the food is probably done.

Definitions

Bake—Cook with dry heat in an oven.

Beat—Blend thoroughly with a beater, whisk, or spoon.

Blend—Combine all ingredients thoroughly.

Boil—Cook in water while liquid bubbles.

Brown—Cook on all sides in a small amount of oil.

Chill—Cool in ice box or refrigerator.

Chop—Cut into small pieces.

Coat—Cover with a thin layer.

Combine—Mix thoroughly.

Cream—Mix all ingredients until creamy.

Cube—Cut into small cubes.

Dice—Cut into small pieces.

Dissolve—Heat or stir until a substance goes into solution.

Fold—Fold one portion of food over with minimum force.

Grate—Move food through small grater opening.

Knead—Work dough by folding and pushing.

Marinate—Place in seasoned liquid.

Mince—Cut into very small pieces.

Mix—Combine ingredients thoroughly.

Oil—Rub inside of Dutch oven or pan with shortening or cooking oil.

Parch—Cook by dry heat.

Peel—Remove skin or peeling of fruit or vegetable.

Poach—Cook in hot liquid.

Roast—Cook with small amount of liquid.

Simmer—Cook in liquid that has a small amount of bubbling (boiling), usually in a covered container.

Sprinkle—Shake small particles on the food.

Steam—Cook in liquid with closed lid to retain steam.

Stew—Cook in liquid, usually with lid on container.

Stir—Mix ingredients with a spoon.

Whip—Blend vigorously with a beater, whisk, or spoon.

WHOLE WHEAT

- When a recipe calls for flour, consider using whole wheat flour rather than white flour. The whole wheat flour will provide more nutrition and will enhance the flavor.

- When you modify a white flour recipe to use whole wheat flour, increase the leavening. I usually double the amount of baking power for this purpose.

- Some people prefer to use a mixture of one-half whole wheat and one-half white flour. This is a way to move into use of the whole wheat product.

FLOUR BARREL

When planning a long camping trip activity, you may want a basic flour mix from which several meal items can be made. The following mixture of dry ingredients can be mixed ahead of time and kept ready for addition of moist ingredients at the needed time for cooking.

5 lb all purpose flour	3 tbsp salt
½ cup sugar	¾ cup baking powder
2¼ cups dry milk	2 lb butter

Mix the flour, milk, baking powder, sugar and salt thoroughly in a large bowl. Then add butter and blend it into the other ingredients until a uniform, crumbly mix is obtained. Store this basic mix in a covered container at room temperature.

Use of Flour Barrel

FOOD ITEM	AMOUNT OF MIX (in cups)	SUGAR (in cups)	EGGS	WATER (in cups)	OTHER	REMARKS	NUMBER OF ITEMS	BAKING TIME (in minutes)
Biscuits	3			3/4		place on oven bottom	20–30	10–15
Pancakes	5		3	3		grill on inverted lid	30–40	
Muffins	3	1/4	1	1		use cupcake holders	16–20	20–25
Cookies	3	1	1	1/4	1 tsp flavoring: almond, vanilla, lemon, or peppermint; 1/2 cup shortening	variations with raisins, nuts, or chocolate drops, drop or roll and cut for pan	30–40	10–15
Coffee cake	3	1	1	1	top with 3/4 cup brown sugar; 4 tbsp butter; 2 tsp cinnamon	blend mixture; pour into oven; cover with topping		30–40
Cake	4	2	2	1 1/3	2 tsp vanilla or other flavoring	beat egg, add to other mix, beat well; pour in oven		30–40

MEATS, FISH & EGGS

BEEF GOULASH

3 lb beef, cubed

2 tbsp cooking oil

1 tsp salt

1 can mushroom soup

Brown beef in the cooking oil in an open oven; add salt and can of soup. Place lid on oven and cook over low fire 1 hour; add water if needed.

Serves 8

Variations

1. Add some chopped carrots or onions.

2. Use vegetable soup instead of mushroom soup.

3. Use 1 can soup and 1 small can of corn.

BEEF BAKE

2 cups uncooked macaroni

$1\frac{1}{2}$ lb ground beef

$\frac{3}{4}$ cup chopped celery

$\frac{1}{2}$ cup chopped bell pepper

1 8-oz can tomato sauce

1 cup water

$\frac{1}{2}$ tsp salt

Cook macaroni, rinse, drain, and set aside. Brown the ground beef, celery and bell peppers; drain well. Add tomato sauce, water, salt and the cooked macaroni; mix well. Place the mixed ingredients into an oiled pan or directly in bottom of oven. Bake for 30 minutes.

Serves 8

Variations

1. Add a 16-oz can of whole kernel corn to the mixed ingredients.

2. Sprinkle grated cheese on the dish before baking.

BEEF RIBS

3 tbsp cooking oil	1 cup chopped celery
3 lb beef short ribs, or at least one rib per person	1 cup green peas
	1 8-oz can tomato sauce
3 tbsp molasses	1 can beef broth
2 tbsp vinegar	½ tsp dried thyme or basil

Heat the cooking oil in the open oven and brown the ribs on all sides. Add the other ingredients and place the lid on the oven. Cook for about 2 hours or until the meat is tender. Occasionally check for adequate liquid; add small amount of water if needed.

Remove the liquid fat with a spoon. The vegetables and broth may be served over the ribs.

Serves 8

RICE AND CORNED BEEF

1½ cups brown rice	½ tsp salt
3 cups water	2 12-oz cans corned beef

Place rice, water and salt into oven and cook for 30 minutes. Slice corned beef, place it on top of rice and cook for 15 more minutes or until rice is done.

Serves 8

GREEN BAR STEW

3 lb beef, cubed	4 carrots, diced
2 tbsp cooking oil	1 medium-sized onion, chopped
1 tsp salt	4 medium-sized potatoes, cubed
1 cup water	1 tbsp parsley flakes

Brown beef in cooking oil in an open oven; then add salt and water; cover and cook 30 minutes. Add carrots and onion and cook 30 minutes. Add potatoes and parsley and cook 30–40 minutes more. Cook over low- to medium-heat fire; add water to retain about one inch of liquid in oven.

Serves 8

GUADALUPE CHILI PIE

2 lb ground beef	$\frac{1}{2}$ tsp chili powder
1 medium-sized onion, chopped	$\frac{1}{2}$ tsp salt
1 tbsp butter	1 8-oz can tomato sauce
1 15-oz can chili beans	2 6-oz pkg corn bread mix

Brown beef and onion in the butter in open oven. Add beans, chili powder, salt and sauce and cook for 15 minutes in covered oven.

Mix the corn bread as directed and add to top of meat and beans. Place lid on oven. Cook for 20–30 minutes, until corn bread is done.

Serves 8

NOODLE CASSEROLE

1 lb noodles or spaghetti	1 can mushroom soup
2 lb ground beef	1 can peas
1 medium-sized onion, chopped	1 tsp salt
2 tbsp cooking oil	½ tsp oregano

Cook noodles in a separate pan by directions on package; drain. Brown meat and onion in oil in skillet; then add soup, peas and seasonings. Place noodles and meat mixture together in casserole bowl or pan. Place in oven and bake ¹/₂ hour.

Serves 8

Variation

Mediterranean Casserole: *Instead of mushroom soup, add small can tomato sauce, ¹/₂ cup water, and ¹/₂ lb Mozzarella cheese (cut into small pieces) to the ingredients.*

Serves 8

COWBOY STEW

2–3 lb ground beef	2 15-oz cans chili beans
1 tbsp butter	

Brown beef in butter in open oven. Add beans and cook slowly 15–20 minutes in covered oven.

Serves 8

Variation

Brown one medium onion, finely chopped, with the beef.

MEAT LOAF

3 lb ground beef

1½ cups cracker crumbs

2 eggs

1 8-oz can tomato sauce

1 onion, chopped

½ cup bell pepper, chopped
or 1 tbsp parsley flakes

1½ tsp salt

¼ tsp marjoram

Mix all ingredients; place in casserole dish or pan. Bake 1 hour in covered oven.

Serves 8

Variations

1. Venison Loaf: *Venison or other meat can be used, if available.*
2. Stuffed Bell Peppers: *Cut 4 large bell peppers in half; remove seeds. Equally divide meat mixture and stuff into pepper halves. Place into bowl or pan and bake 1 hour.*

POT ROAST

1 3-lb beef roast—rolled, pot, round bone or rump cut

2 tbsp cooking oil

1 cup water

garlic salt

Brown roast on each side in the oil in open oven. Add water to oven; sprinkle garlic salt on top of roast.

Cook about 2 hours in covered oven, adding small amount of water, if needed.

Serves 8

QUICK CASSEROLE

1 1-oz pkg gravy mix   1 4-oz can of mushrooms
1 12-oz can roast beef   1 8-oz can of water chestnuts
½ cup chopped celery   1 cup rice
1 tbsp minced onion   2 cups water

Mix gravy package in bowl; add beef, celery, onion, mushrooms and water chestnuts. Add rice and water, then place in oven.

Bake 20–25 minutes or until rice is cooked.

Serves 6–8

SWISS STEAK

1 3-lb round steak, 1-inch thick   3 sticks of celery, chopped
3 tbsp butter   ½ cup catsup
1 tsp salt   1 tbsp dried parsley flakes
1 large onion, chopped

Brown both sides of beef in butter in open oven. Add other ingredients to oven and cook covered for 2 hours. Add small amount of water, if needed, to keep sauce thinner.

Serves 8

PORK CHOPS

8 pork chops   1 can mushroom soup
2 tbsp cooking oil   ½ tsp salt

Brown pork chops in oil in open oven. Add soup and salt and cook for 30 minutes in covered oven.

Serves 8

Variations

1. Add 1 can tomato sauce.
2. Add 1 tbsp dried parsley flakes.

HAM AND SWEET POTATOES

¼ cup butter

¾ cup brown sugar

8 slices ham

4 medium-sized sweet
    potatoes

If the ham slices are raw, the ham should be browned in a skillet. Use a small amount of cooking oil and brown the ham on both sides. If the ham is precooked, it may be placed in the oven without further cooking.

Place butter and brown sugar into the oven and stir until well-mixed. Place the thick ham slices into the mixture, one slice for each person.

Peel sweet potatoes and slice the potatoes in ½-inch thick slices. Place sweet potatoes in oven and put the lid on the oven. Bake about 30–40 minutes, or until the potatoes are soft to the prongs of a fork.

Serves 8

PIZZA

1½ lb ground beef

1½ pkg pizza mix

½ lb cheese, grated

olives, sliced

Brown beef in open skillet and set aside (keep the beef warm). Mix pizza dough as directed and divide into 8 equal portions. Form these portions into crust pieces about the size of doughnuts, or a size that allows placing all 8 crusts into two ovens.

Place the ground beef and cheese on the crusts; pour tomato sauce from pizza mix on each crust; then add sliced olives on top.

Bake as directed, or about 25–30 minutes.

Serves 8

Variations

1. Use sausage instead of beef.

2. Place chopped pieces of pimento or parsley on top of sauce.

BATTER DIP

1 egg	½ cup milk or water
½ tsp salt	½ cup flour

Beat ingredients in mixing bowl. Dip your food in this mix and cook in cooking oil.

FISH CHOWDER

3 tbsp cooking oil	1 tsp salt
¼ cup chopped onion	¼ tsp thyme
½ cup chopped bell pepper	¼ tsp chopped basil
1 cup chopped celery	1 tbsp parsley
½ cup chopped carrots	2 lb fish fillets, cut in
1 cup water	small pieces

Heat cooking oil in oven; brown onion, bell pepper, celery and carrots. Add water, salt, thyme, basil and parsley. Cover and cook for 20 minutes. Add fish and cook about 10 minutes or until fish is done. Serve fish and spoon on the sauce.

Serves 8

FISH-IN-FOIL

Fish fillets, one per person

For each serving:

2 tbsp chopped carrots	1 tsp dried parsley
1 thin slice of lemon	

Place a fillet on a sheet of heavy-duty aluminum foil, and lay the other ingredients on the fillet. Bring foil edges together and seal the foil edges by folding them twice. Make a separate foil package for each person.

Bake foil packs in oven for about 20 minutes or until fish meat flakes well. You may want to limit an oven to three or four foil packs and use an additional oven for other foil packages.

CATFISH PARMESAN

Crumbs for topping:

2 cups dry bread crumbs	1 tsp salt
¾ cup grated Parmesan cheese	¼ cup cooking oil or
4 tbsp chopped parsley	melted butter
½ tsp oregano	4 serving-size pieces of
½ tsp chopped basil	catfish fillets

Mix the topping crumbs well and place in a shallow pan. Place the cooking oil or butter in a small bowl.

Dip each fillet piece in the bowl of oil and then dip each piece in the dry crumb mix. Place the fillet pieces in an oiled pan and place the pan in the oven.

Bake the pan of fish for about 25 minutes or until the meat flakes easily. Test for doneness.

Serves 4

SALMON BAKE

1 10¾-oz can cream of mushroom soup

1 15½-oz can salmon, drained

½ cup chopped celery

¼ cup sliced green olives

1 tbsp soy sauce

1 3-oz can of chow mein noodles

Combine soup, crumbled salmon, celery, olives and soy sauce in bowl. Mix and place into oiled baking pan or directly in bottom of oven. Cook for 15 minutes. Add noodles and bake an additional 15 minutes.

Serves 8

Variation

Instead of noodles, prepare biscuit dough, cut and place biscuits on top of mixed ingredients.

BAKED EGGS

1 egg per person

Crack and pour an egg into an oiled dessert mold, foil cupcake pan, or constructed foil holder. This constructed foil holder can be made of a piece of heavy aluminum foil pressed around a 10- to 12-oz can, then removed to serve as your egg holder. You may want to put cupcake papers into the mold or foil pan, then remove the egg in cupcake paper when done.

Place egg containers in oven and bake for about 10 minutes to the preferred consistency.

Eggs can be prepared for individual preferences and you may wish to enhance the eggs by adding one of the following ingredients before baking:

crumbled, crisp bacon   salt, pepper
dill weed   Italian seasoning
grated cheese

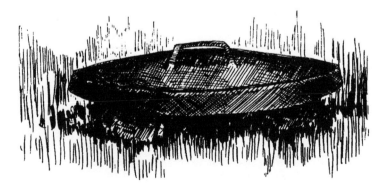

BEEF-N-EGGS

2 15-oz cans of corned beef hash   8 eggs

Divide the corned beef into eight equal portions, press the beef on the sides and bottom of oiled dessert molds or foil cup cake pan. You may want to place cupcake papers in aluminum dessert molds and use these for holding your beef and egg.

Break eggs and place one egg into the beef-lined bowls. Place the bowls in the oven and bake for 15 minutes. Using two ovens with four bowls in each oven works well.

Serves 8

EGGS-IN-A-BOX

thick-sliced bread   ½ cup butter
eggs

Using biscuit cutter, cut hole in center of thick-sliced bread. Soften butter and spread on each side of bread.

Place bread in bottom of open oven until one side of bread is toasted. Turn bread over and slowly pour one egg into the hole in each piece of bread; place lid on oven and cook eggs for about 5 minutes and remove each egg-in-a-box with flat lifter.

You may wish to use an additional oven to speed preparation of the meal for all persons.

SALMON-BROCCOLI PIE

¾ cup brown rice

1½ cups water

1 tsp cooking oil

⅛ tsp salt

¼ cup salad dressing

2 tbsp Dijon-style mustard

1 cup cheddar cheese, grated

1 14-oz can salmon

1 6-oz can water chestnuts,
   drained and chopped

1 cup broccoli, chopped

2 eggs, beaten

2 tsp milk

Combine rice, water, cooking oil and salt. Bring to a boil, lower heat and simmer for about 45 minutes, or until rice is cooked.

Mix the cooked rice, salad dressing, mustard and cheese. Press this mixture in the bottom and sides of an oiled 9-inch pie pan. Bake this crust in an oven for 10 minutes.

Remove the pie pan. Drain the salmon and cut it in small pieces. Place the cut salmon, chopped water chestnuts and chopped broccoli in the crust. Stir the eggs and milk and pour over the pie filling.

Bake the pie for 40 minutes in a moderate oven and remove to cool for 15 minutes. Cut into slices.

Serves 6–8

FISH FILLETS AND RICE

4 fish fillets

2 lemons

2 tbsp cooking oil

1 cup brown rice

2 cups water

1 tbsp cooking oil

¼ tsp salt

dill weed

I prefer to use catfish fillets, but you might wish to use any single-serving size fillets. Cut the fillets in half for a more manageable size to cook and serve. Place the juice of the lemons and the cooking oil in a bowl and add the fillets to marinate several hours before cooking. The bowl can be covered and refrigerated in an ice cooler until needed.

Combine the rice, water, cooking oil and salt in a heavy, covered cooking pan or Dutch oven; bring to a boil and simmer for about 25 minutes. Remove the lid and quickly place the pieces of fish on top of the rice. Sprinkle dill weed on top of the fish.

Cover the pan or oven and cook an additional 15–20 minutes, until the rice and fish are done.

Serve the rice on plates, placing the fish on top of the rice servings.

Serves 4

Variation

Add chopped basil leaves or chopped parsley flakes to the marinade.

MEAT MARINADE

1 cup cooking oil   ½ tsp garlic salt
½ cup vinegar

Variations

1. Add 2 tbsp Worcestershire sauce.
2. Add 1 tbsp chopped onions.

Notes

Notes

VEGETABLES & SOUPS

STEAMED RICE

3 cups water	1 tsp salt
1½ cups rice	1 tbsp cooking oil

Bring water to a boil in the oven. Place other ingredients in oven. Cover and cook over low heat about 20–25 minutes, or until water is absorbed.

Serves 8

SUCCOTASH

½ lb dried lima beans	water
¼ lb salt pork, diced	1 12-oz can kernel corn or
½ tsp salt	fresh corn

Cover beans with water and soak overnight; then drain.

Place beans, pork, salt and enough water to cover the beans and pork in the oven. Cook covered over low fire for $1^{1}/_{2}$ hours; add small amount of water if needed. Add corn; stir and cook $^{1}/_{2}$ hour.

Serves 8

PINTO BEANS

2 cups beans, dried	1 tsp onion salt
water	¼ lb salt pork, sliced

Place beans in 6 cups of water and soak overnight.

Put onion salt and pork in the beans; cover and cook 3 hours. Add small amounts of water if needed.

Serves 8

OZARK BAKED BEANS

2 cups white beans, dried	1 tsp dry mustard
1½ qt water	¼ cup molasses
1 tsp salt	¼ lb salt pork, sliced
⅓ cup brown sugar	1 small onion, sliced

Place beans in water and soak overnight.

Add salt and cook for 1 hour or until tender. Drain liquid into a separate pan. Add other ingredients and 2 cups of drained liquid to beans. Cover and bake for 2–3 hours. Check occasionally, adding small amounts of water if needed.

Serves 8

CABBAGE

2 medium heads cabbage	1 cup water
1 tsp salt	vinegar

Cut heads of cabbage in quarters; place in salted boiled water. Cover and cook 10–15 minutes. Test for tenderness; do not overcook. Individuals can season with vinegar to taste.

Serves 8

CORN ON THE COB

1 ear corn per person   boiling water
1 tsp salt

Remove shucks and silk from ears. Place corn in oven; add salt and enough boiling water to cover corn. Cook 8–10 minutes in covered oven. Puncture corn grains with knife tip to test for tenderness.

BAKED CORN

1 16-oz can cream-style corn	2 cups grated cheese
1 16-oz can whole kernel corn	1 tsp baking powder
½ cup cornmeal	¼ cup cooking oil
1 tbsp garlic salt	2 eggs, beaten

Combine corn, cornmeal, garlic salt, cheese, baking powder and cooking oil. Beat eggs and add to mixture. Place mixture into baking pan or directly in oven.

Bake 40–50 minutes.

Serves 8

Variation

Add 4-oz can chopped chilies or ¹/₂ cup chopped bell peppers.

BAKED POTATOES

1 potato per person

Wash the outside of the potatoes, and puncture a small hole on two sides of each potato.

Place potatoes in the oven, cover and cook about 1 hour. The time will vary depending on the size of the potatoes.

POTATO CUBES

4 large potatoes, cubed

2 tbsp lemon juice

4 tbsp cooking oil

¼ tsp garlic salt

2 tsp sweet basil, chopped

If potato skins are soft, do not peel potatoes; if the skins are tough, peel potatoes. Cut the potatoes into cubes and place in a bowl.

Combine the lemon juice, cooking oil, garlic salt and basil. Pour this mixture on the potato cubes and stir to spread the seasoning on the cubes.

Place the cubes in an oiled baking pan, then put the pan in a heated oven. Bake the potatoes for about 20 minutes, stir the potatoes and bake them 20 more minutes, if needed.

Remove the pan and serve warm.

Serves 4–6

HERBED POTATOES

3 lb potatoes

3 cups boiling water

1 can cream of mushroom soup

1 tsp basil

½ tsp marjoram

2 tbsp butter

1 cup cracker crumbs

1 tbsp Parmesan cheese

Peel and cube potatoes. In a pan, place potatoes in the boiling water; cook about 12–15 minutes until potatoes are almost soft. Drain water and place potatoes in an oiled baking pan.

In a separate pan, mix the soup, basil and marjoram. Heat the mixture 4–5 minutes and pour it over the potatoes.

In another pan, melt the butter, stir in the cracker crumbs and cheese. Pour this mixture over the potatoes.

Bake about 15 minutes.

Serves 8

BROCCOLI

2 cups boiling water   2 lb broccoli

Wash fresh broccoli; cut the flowering top into large pieces and the stalk into one-inch pieces. Place 2 cups of boiling water in oven; then add the broccoli pieces.

Cover oven and cook about 5–6 minutes or until tender; do not overcook. Serve with a tablespoon of butter.

Serves 8

BRUSSELS SPROUTS

2 cups boiling water   2 lb brussels sprouts

Place 2 cups of boiling water in oven. Wash brussels sprouts and place in boiling water.

Cover oven and cook about 8–10 minutes or until tender; do not overcook. Serve with a tablespoon of butter.

Serves 8

NOODLE BAKE

1 lb noodles, cooked   1 tsp salt

2 cups yogurt   1 cup cracker crumbs

2 eggs, beaten

Cook noodles; then place them into an oiled baking pan or directly in the oven. Mix yogurt, eggs and salt in a bowl and pour over the noodles. Sprinkle cracker crumbs on top.

Bake about 15 minutes.

Serves 8

DILLED CARROTS

4 tbsp butter	2 tbsp chopped fresh dill or
4 cups sliced carrots	dried dill weed
½ cup water	

Melt butter in bottom of oven. Add carrots, water, dill, and stir. Place lid on oven and bake for about 10 minutes.

Serves 8

CHEESE GRITS

6 cups boiling water	½ cup butter
1 tsp salt	1 lb grated cheese
1½ cup grits	3 eggs

Stir grits into salted, boiling water for 5 minutes. Add butter and cheese, stir and remove to cool for 5 minutes. Beat eggs and stir in grits.

Place in oiled baking dish and bake for 40 minutes.

Serves 8

Variations

1. Add 2 tbsp chopped pimento with the cheese.
2. Add 2 tbsp chopped bell peppers with the cheese.

BAKED SQUASH

4 small acorn squash	butter

Wash squash, cut in half and remove seeds. Place halves in bottom of oven with cut sides up. You might need two ovens for adequate space. Place a teaspoon of butter in each squash half.

Bake for about 15–20 minutes; check doneness with knife blade.

Serves 8

Variations

1. Use butternut squash.
2. Sprinkle squash halves with dill weed.
3. Sprinkle squash halves with nutmeg.

SQUASH BAKE

4 tbsp butter	1 cup cracker crumbs
2 lb yellow squash	¼ lb cheese, grated
¼ tsp salt	

Melt butter and place into oiled baking dish or directly in oven. Place sliced squash and salt in butter; place cheese and then cracker crumbs on top.

Bake for about 10 minutes until tender to fork. Do not overcook.

Serves 8

Variation

Sprinkle Italian seasoning with the cracker crumbs.

STIRRED VEGETABLES

¼ cup butter	1 cup carrots, sliced
½ cup chopped onion	1 tsp garlic salt
2 cups cauliflower, cut up	1 tsp parsley
2 cups zucchini squash, sliced	½ tsp chopped basil

Melt butter in bottom of oven. Brown onion, add other ingredients, and stir occasionally for 5 minutes. Place lid oil oven and cook about 8–10 minutes or until done.

Serves 8

Variation

Sprinkle with dill weed.

VEGETABLE-CHEESE CASSEROLE

2 medium eggplants

4 cups boiling, salted water

1 egg

1 cup cottage cheese

1 tbsp Italian seasoning

1 10¾-oz can cream of
    mushroom soup

4 oz Mozzarella or soft cheese

1 cup cracker crumbs

Wash and peel eggplants; cut into cubes. Place eggplant in a pan of boiling water to cover, cook about 5 minutes until tender. Drain water and place eggplant in an oiled pan. Beat egg and stir egg, cottage cheese, seasoning and soup with eggplant. Slice soft cheese and place on top, sprinkle on cracker crumbs and bake for about 30 minutes.

Serves 8

Variation

Use 8-oz can of tomato sauce instead of mushroom soup.

ZUCCHINI BAKE

1 cup brown rice

3 medium zucchini squash

1 large tomato

½ lb cheese

2 cups sour cream or yogurt

½ tsp garlic salt

1 tsp oregano

1 tbsp parsley

Cook brown rice and place in oiled pan. Slice zucchini and tomato; place on top of rice. Grate cheese and sprinkle on top.

Mix sour cream, garlic salt, oregano and parsley and pour on top. Bake 30 minutes.

Serves 8

BACON-SPINACH PIE

1 9-in. pie crust
½ lb bacon
1 cup cheese, grated
1 10-oz pkg spinach or
   1 can spinach, drained

½ cup cracker crumbs
3 eggs
1½ cups milk

Prepare pie crust, bake for 5 minutes and set aside. Cook bacon until crisp; drain and crumble. Mix bacon, cheese, spinach and cracker crumbs. Beat eggs; combine with milk and add to mixed ingredients. Pour mixture into the pie crust.

Bake pie 50–60 minutes in oven. Remove pie from oven and cool 15 minutes.

Serves 6–8

Variation
Add sliced mushrooms to mixture.

POPCORN

butter
popcorn

salt

Melt 4 oz (one stick) of butter in oven. Cover most of bottom of the oven with one layer of popcorn. Place lid on the oven, and bake until the sounds indicate all the corn has popped; during the popping time, you should lift the oven by the bail and rotate the oven to better stir the whole batch of corn.

Pour popped corn into a paper bag; pour additional melted butter and salt for desired taste. Shake the bag to distribute salt and serve while warm.

TOASTED PECANS

butter   salt

pecan halves

Melt a few tablespoons of butter in oven and add pecan halves. Rub some butter on pecan halves; salt if desired.

Place the lid on the oven and bake for 15–20 minutes. Remove pecans and serve while warm.

Variations

1. Sprinkle pecans with sugar instead of salt.

2. Sprinkle cinnamon with the sugar.

PARCHED PEANUTS

peanuts in shells

Place 1 to 2 pounds of unshelled peanuts in oven. Cover with lid and bake about 40–50 minutes. During baking, occasionally stir peanuts to heat the whole batch evenly; test for doneness during the baking. Serve while warm.

SPLIT PEA SOUP

2 cups dry split peas   1 small onion, chopped

¼ lb bacon, diced   1 tsp salt

2½ cups water

Place peas in 2$^1/_2$ cups water and soak overnight. Brown bacon and crumble it. Add bacon, salt and onion to the peas. Cover and cook over slow fire for 1 hour.

Inspect occasionally, adding small amounts of water, if needed, to thin the soup while it cooks. Serve with crackers.

Serves 8

GUMBO

2 lb beef	1 16-oz can tomatoes
½ cup flour	1 large bell pepper, chopped
4 tsp butter	1 10-oz pkg frozen okra
1 tsp salt	1 tsp thyme
2 qt water	1 tsp tarragon
1 large onion, chopped	1 bay leaf

Cut meat into small cubes; roll in flour and brown in butter in open oven. Add salt, water and chopped onion; cover and cook for 1 hour.

Add tomatoes, bell pepper, okra, thyme, tarragon and bay leaf and cook slowly for 1–2 hours.

Serves 8

Variation

Gulf Coast Gumbo: *Use fish, shrimp or crabmeat instead of beef. Add 1 tsp gumbo filé.*

LENTIL-RICE STEW

2 tbsp butter	1 can beef soup
¼ cup minced onion	¾ cup brown rice
1 cup diced celery	(not minute or processed)
6 cups water	1½ tsp garlic salt
1 cup dried lentils	½ tsp chopped basil
¾ cup diced carrots	½ tsp oregano

Melt butter in oven; stir and brown onions and celery. Add water and lentils. Place lid on oven, bring to a boil, and cook 20 minutes. Add other ingredients, bring to a boil, and cook 1 hour, or until rice is done. A small amount of water may be added, if necessary.

Serves 6–8

VEGETABLE STEW

1 lb ground beef	1 cup chopped bell peppers
2 cups chopped celery	1 tsp salt
1 cup chopped onions	1 tsp sugar
2 cups sliced zucchini	1 tsp Italian seasoning
1 cup sliced yellow squash	½ tsp chopped basil
2 16-oz cans tomatoes	

Brown beef, celery and onion in an open oven; drain well. Add zucchini, squash, tomatoes, bell peppers and seasonings. Cover with lid and cook 30–40 minutes. Add small amount of water, if needed.

Serves 8

POTATO SOUP

2 tbsp butter	2 cups water
1 cup diced celery	3 cups milk
¼ cup chopped onions	2 tsp salt
4 cups diced potatoes	2 tbsp parsley

Melt butter and brown the celery and onions. Add potatoes and water; then cook with lid on for about 1 hour. Mash vegetables for smoothness. Add milk, salt and parsley, and simmer again for 15 minutes.

Serves 8

Variations

    1. Add finely chopped carrots.
    2. Add finely chopped ham or bacon pieces.

Notes

Notes

Notes

DESSERTS

PINEAPPLE UPSIDE-DOWN CAKE

¼ cup butter

½ cup brown sugar

1 can sliced pineapple

1 pkg yellow cake mix

1 egg

Place butter and brown sugar in the oven and stir until well mixed. Place the pineapple slices in the butter and sugar mixture in the bottom of the oven.

In a separate bowl, mix the cake mix and the egg as directed on the package. Pour this batter over the pineapple in the oven, then put the lid on the oven and bake about 30–40 minutes. Test cake for doneness with a straw.

When the cake is done, remove the coals from the oven, remove the lid, and let the oven cool for about 10 minutes. Using a large cutting board or a piece of corrugated cardboard covered with waxed paper, hold the board on top of the oven and invert the oven quickly. This will allow the cake to fall on the board and the pineapple will be on the top. A safer way to support the cake when you invert it is to cut the cardboard in a round piece the same size as the cake, and it will fit inside the oven on the cake; then when the oven is inverted, the cardboard can be held directly under the cake.

Serves 8

Variations
1. Cherries may be placed with the pineapple to provide color.
2. Crushed pineapple may be used for a more uniform topping.

LAZY COBBLER

1 large can sliced peaches	butter
1 pkg white cake mix	cinnamon

When oven is preheated, pour the whole can of peaches and juice into oven. Then add the dry cake mix on top of the peaches. Place several pieces of butter on top, and sprinkle cinnamon over all. Place lid on oven and bake about 45 minutes. Recipe will give a layer of peaches with a cake covering.

Serves 8

Variations
1. Stir the cake mix and peaches when placed in oven to provide a more spongy layer of cake.
2. Use canned apples instead of peaches, and add 1 tbsp cinnamon to the apples.
3. Use canned cherries instead of peaches, and add more sugar with the cherries.
4. Instead of the white cake mix, use a yellow or spice cake mix.

TRAIL COBBLER

2 cups biscuit mix	1 cup butter
2 cups sugar	1 can fruit, drained
2 cups milk or water	

Mix the biscuit mix, sugar, milk and butter. Add fruit and stir. Bake in covered oven about 1 hour.

Serves 8

CARNIVAL APPLES

apples	raisins
sugar	cinnamon

Use tart apples such as Winesap, Jonathon, or Rome Beauty, if available. Cut cylindrical core from apples and place apples in a pan. In the core hole of each apple, place sugar, raisins and cinnamon. Place pan in oven; cover and bake about 30 minutes.

QUICK CINNAMON ROLLS

2 6-oz pkg biscuit mix	1 cup brown sugar
3–4 oz raisins	cinnamon

Mix the biscuit mix as directed and pat out in a rectangular shape on a floured, flat surface. Spread raisins and brown sugar over the dough. Sprinkle with cinnamon. Beginning with one long side of the dough, with floured hands, roll the dough into a cylinder. Cut slices from this rolled cylinder and place in bottom of oven. Place lid on oven and bake about 15–20 minutes.

Serves 8

GINGERBREAD

$\frac{1}{2}$ cup butter	1 tsp soda
1 cup brown sugar	$\frac{1}{2}$ tsp salt
1 egg	$\frac{1}{2}$ tsp ginger
$\frac{1}{2}$ cup molasses	1 tsp cinnamon
$1\frac{1}{2}$ cups flour	$\frac{1}{2}$ tsp allspice
$\frac{1}{2}$ cup hot water	$\frac{1}{4}$ tsp cloves

Cream butter, sugar and egg. Blend in molasses and water. Add other dry ingredients and stir to mix dough. Put in greased pan and place in the oven or pour the batter into the oven and bake about 30–40 minutes, testing for doneness.

Serves 8

SOPAPILLAS

1 envelope dry yeast	1 tbsp cooking oil
½ cup warm water	1 tsp sugar
3 cups flour	cooking oil
1 egg	sugar
½ tsp salt	cinnamon
honey	

Dissolve yeast in the warm water, mix with other ingredients. Knead for several minutes and set aside in a warm place until dough doubles (about 2 hours). Roll flat, cut into $1^1/_2$-inch squares, and allow to rise again for 1 hour.

Drop squares into deep cooking oil and cook to a golden brown, turning once. Drain the squares briefly when you remove them from oil; then turn them over in sugar and cinnamon mixture. Serve hot with honey.

Makes about 50

TRAIL DOUGHNUTS

3 cups flour	½ tsp cinnamon
1 cup sugar	½ tsp nutmeg
½ tsp salt	¾ cup milk
1 tsp baking powder	2 eggs
1 tsp butter	cooking oil

Frosting:

sugar	cinnamon

Mix all seven of the dry ingredients, then slowly add milk while stirring. Add 2 eggs to the batter and stir well.

On a floured surface, roll or pat out the dough to a thickness of $^3/_8$-inch and cut out the doughnuts in 2-inch squares.

Place cooking oil in the oven for deep frying. Place the doughnuts in the heated oil, cook on one side and turn once to cook on the other side.

Remove each doughnut when it is cooked, and drain it briefly.

In a separate pan or paper bag, place some sugar and cinnamon for a frosting dip. After each doughnut is drained, it can be dipped or turned in the sugar and cinnamon mixture for a frosting.

Makes about 50

BIZCOCHITOS

1 cup butter	1½ tsp baking powder
1 cup sugar	½ tsp salt
1 tsp anise seed	¼ cup water
1 egg	cinnamon
3 cups flour	sugar

Blend butter, sugar and anise seed. Beat egg and add to the mixture. Add flour, baking powder, salt and water and mix well. Roll dough on a floured surface and cut out cookie shapes. Place these cookies in a pan and sprinkle the top of each cookie with a mixture of cinnamon and sugar; this should be in a ratio of 1 tsp cinnamon to 3 tbsp sugar.

Place the pan in a covered oven and bake for 15–20 minutes. The cookies should be thin and crisp.

Makes about 50

BUTTER BARS

2 sticks butter	2 cups flour
1 lb brown sugar	2 tsp baking powder
1 cup sugar	½ tsp salt
4 eggs	1 tsp vanilla

Blend butter and sugars; add eggs; and beat. Add other dry ingredients and stir until well mixed. Pour into a greased, floured pan and place in the oven.

Cook 30–40 minutes and remove from oven. Allow the pan to cool for 10 minutes, cut in rectangular bars and serve warm.

Makes 15–20

PECAN DROPS

1 cup butter	2 tsp vanilla
⅓ cup sugar	2 cups flour
2 tsp water	1 cup pecans, chopped and toasted

Blend butter and sugar. Add water and vanilla and mix well. Add flour and pecans and stir to a smooth batter. Drop spoonfuls of batter on a greased pan and place pan in the oven; or drop the spoonfuls of batter directly on the bottom of the oven.

Place the lid on the oven and bake about 15 minutes.

Makes about 50

CRISP SUGAR COOKIES

¾ cup butter, softened	1 tsp almond flavoring
¾ cup sugar	2¼ cups flour
⅛ tsp salt	water
1 egg	sugar

Cream butter, sugar and salt in a bowl. Stir in egg and almond flavoring. Gradually add flour and stir until the dough is thoroughly blended. If dough is too stiff, add a tablespoon of water and mix in the dough.

Place the dough in an air-tight wrapper or container, and chill for 2 hours, if possible.

Roll the dough on a floured surface to a ¼-inch thickness. Cut out cookies with a small cookie cutter and place them in an oiled pan. Sprinkle a small amount of sugar on top of each cookie.

Place the pan in a moderately hot oven and bake 12 to 15 minutes.

Makes about 50

Variations

1. *Use 1 cup of whole wheat flour and 1 ¼ cups of white flour instead of 2 ¼ cups of flour.*
2. *Use lemon flavoring instead of almond flavoring.*

OATMEAL COOKIES

½ cup butter	½ tsp salt
¾ cup brown sugar	1 tsp baking powder
1 egg	½ tsp cinnamon
¼ cup milk	½ tsp nutmeg
1 cup flour	1½ cups quick oats

Blend butter, sugar and egg; then mix in milk. Add the dry ingredients and stir to a smooth mixture. Drop spoonfuls of batter on a greased pan and place pan in the oven; or drop the spoonfuls of batter directly on bottom of the oven. Place lid on the oven and bake about 15 minutes.

Makes about 40

Variation

Add ½ cup raisins.

CRUMB APPLE CAKE

2 cups flour	2 eggs
½ cup sugar	2 large tart apples, sliced
½ tsp salt	⅔ cup brown sugar
1 pkg yeast	½ cup flour
½ cup milk	1 tbsp cinnamon
½ cup butter	6 tbsp butter

In a bowl, mix 1 cup flour, sugar, salt and yeast. Add warmed milk and mix well. Add butter, eggs and the other 1 cup of flour and mix well. Pour batter into greased pan and place sliced apples on top of batter.

Combine brown sugar, flour, cinnamon and butter in separate bowl. Mix until crumbly. Sprinkle this crumbly mix over apples and set pan aside in a warm place for 1 hour.

Bake about 30–40 minutes.

Serves 8

Variations

    1. Add 1 tsp nutmeg to batter.
    2. Instead of apples, use 1 1/2 cups blueberries, cherries or other fruit,
       drained.

PEPPERMINT POUND CAKE

1 cups butter	1/2 tsp salt
2 cups sugar	3 cups flour
4 eggs	3/4 cup buttermilk
2 tsp peppermint extract	1/2 cup peppermint candy,
1 tsp butter flavoring	crushed

Cream butter and sugar. Add eggs and beat well. Mix in extract, flavoring and salt. Add flour and buttermilk in small amounts, stirring well. When batter is thoroughly mixed, add crushed candy and stir gently throughout.

    Pour in oven, cover and bake for about 1 hour. Test for doneness with straw.

Serves 8

SPICE CAKE

1 pkg spice cake mix	3–4 oz raisins

Mix cake mix as directed; stir in raisins and pour batter into oiled oven. Cover and bake about 30–35 minutes. Test for doneness with straw.

HILL COUNTRY COFFEE CAKE

2 1/4 cups flour	3/4 cup sugar
1/2 tsp salt	1/2 cup cooking oil
1 tsp baking powder	1 egg, beaten
1 tbsp cinnamon	1 cup milk
1 cup brown sugar	

Combine the flour, salt, baking powder and cinnamon and mix well. Add brown and white sugars and mix well. Add the cooking oil, egg and milk; stir the mixture until well mixed. Pour the batter into an oiled baking pan and place the pan in the oven.

Bake for 30–35 minutes in covered oven; then test for doneness.

Serves 8

Variations

1. *Sprinkle $^1/_2$ cup chopped pecans on top of batter after the pan is placed in the oven.*
2. *After cake is removed from the oven, pour a mixture of confectioners' sugar and milk on top of the cake.*
3. *Add 1 tsp lemon flavoring to batter.*
4. *Sprinkle a mixture of brown sugar and flour on top of the batter after it is poured into the pan.*
5. *Use 1 cup of whole wheat flour and $1^1/_4$ cups of white flour.*

PIE CRUST

2 cups flour	$^2/_3$ cup butter
1 tsp salt	4–6 tbsp water

Blend flour, salt and butter. Slowly mix in water, stirring with fork.

Divide dough and, on a floured surface, pat or roll to needed size, allowing about 60% of the dough for the bottom crust. Place the bottom crust in a floured pan and then pour the fruit or other filling in the bottom crust. The top crust or lattice strip dough can be patted or rolled on a floured surface, trimmed to desired size, and placed on the top of the filling so that the edges of both crusts overlap. Dampen the edges of both crusts with a few drops of water and seal the two crusts together by pinching with the fingers or using a wet fork.

FRESH FRUIT COBBLER

4 cups fresh fruit

1 cup sugar

pie crust (see page 63)

2 tbsp cornstarch

¼ cup water

1 tsp almond flavoring

(optional)

This can be an opportunity to use fresh blackberries, blueberries, huckleberries or raspberries that are available. You might also use fresh strawberries or peaches.

Combine the fresh fruit, sugar, cornstarch and water in a pan and heat for 10 minutes on low heat. Stir occasionally during the cooking.

Prepare the pie crust using 60% of the dough for lower crust. Roll the dough on a floured surface and place this crust in an oiled baking dish. Pour the cooked fruit mixture on this crust and place the upper crust on top. You can seal the two crusts together, if they are adequate in size. The cobbler can have only the lower crust in the bottom of the dish and the upper crust on the top of the fruit mixture.

Using a knife blade, punch decorative slots into the upper crust. Bake for 45–50 minutes in an oven.

Serves 6–8

FRUIT PIE

pie crust (see page 63)   1 can pie filling

Mix pie crust as directed. Shape to form upper and lower round pie crusts, or use 1 crust for bottom and make $1/2$-inch wide strips of other crust to lace across top of pie for top crust. Place lower crust in floured pie pan.

Place fruit filling in bottom crust; cover with top crust. Bake 20–30 minutes in a covered oven until brown.

Serves 8

FOLDED PIES

pie crust (see page 63)	butter
flour	sugar
raisins	

Mix pie crust as directed and divide into 8 equal portions. Pat each portion into a round crust piece on a flat, floured surface. Place some raisins, a small piece of butter and sugar on the middle of each piece. Fold the dough piece in half, enveloping the ingredients, and pinch the semicircle edges together or seal using a wet fork. To assure a seal, wet the edges of the crust before pressing together.

Place in covered oven and bake about 20–30 minutes, until crust is golden brown.

Serves 8

PECAN PIES

Crust:

1 3-oz pkg cream cheese	1 cup flour
½ cup butter	

Soften cream cheese and butter; blend with flour. Divide dough into 8 equal portions. Roll or pat out dough to fit cupcake baking pans. Press dough to bottom and sides of cupcake pans.

Filling:

½ cup brown sugar	1 tbsp milk
¼ cup sugar	1 tsp vanilla
1 tbsp flour	¼ cup butter, melted
1 egg	½ cup toasted chopped pecans

Mix sugars and flour. Beat in egg, milk, vanilla and butter. Stir in chopped pecans. Pour mixture into the crust-lined pans.

Bake in oven 35–40 minutes. Remove pies and let them cool; then remove from pans.

Serves 8

CHESS PIE

¾ cup brown sugar
¾ cup sugar
1 tsp flour
2 eggs
1 tsp lemon flavoring

2 tbsp milk
½ cup butter, melted
1 cup toasted chopped pecans
(optional)

Mix sugars and flour. Beat in eggs, lemon flavoring, milk and butter. Stir in pecans, if desired. Pour mixture into pie crust.

Bake in oven 40–45 minutes. Remove and let pie cool.

Serves 8

Variations

1. Instead of pecans, use one 8-oz can of crushed pineapple, drained.
2. Instead of lemon flavoring, use vanilla.

LEMON BARS

Crust:

1 cup whole wheat flour
1¼ cup flour

½ cup powdered sugar
1 cup butter, softened

Filling:

4 eggs, beaten
2 cups sugar
⅓ cup lemon juice

¼ cup flour
½ tsp baking powder

Crust: Stir flours and sugar together in a mixing bowl. Mix in butter until thoroughly blended. Press the flour mixture on the bottom of an oiled baking pan. Bake in oven for 25–30 minutes until the crust is lightly brown.

Filling: Combine eggs, sugar and lemon juice; beat well. Mix flour and baking powder in a separate bowl and stir into the egg and sugar mixture.

Pour this mixture over the baked crust and bake this combination in oven for 25 minutes.

Remove the pan from the oven and allow it to cool. If desired, sift powdered sugar on top of the filling. Cut into bars or squares.

Makes 15–20

SOUR CREAM POUND CAKE

1 cup butter	½ tsp salt
3 cups sugar	½ tsp soda
4 eggs	3 cups flour
1 tsp vanilla extract	1 cup sour cream
1 tsp almond extract	

Cream butter and sugar. Add eggs and beat well. Mix in extracts, salt and soda. Add flour and sour cream in small amounts, stirring well. Place into oiled baking pan or directly in oven.

Bake for 50–60 minutes.

Serves 8 to 10

Variation

Sprinkle confectioners' sugar on cake after removing it from oven.

PEANUT BUTTER NUGGETS

1 cup peanut butter	1 egg
1 cup sugar	1 tsp vanilla

Put ingredients in a bowl and mix well. Spoon the dough into balls about 1 inch in diameter. Place these on an oiled pan or the oiled bottom of the oven. Flatten the dough balls with a floured fork. You may cook in multiple batches or use several ovens.

Bake about 15 minutes.

Makes about 40

PEANUT BUTTER COOKIES

½ cup peanut butter	½ tsp vanilla
½ cup butter	1¼ cups flour
1 cup sugar	½ tsp baking powder
1 cup brown sugar	½ tsp soda
1 egg	¼ tsp salt

Cream peanut butter, butter and sugars. Then mix in egg and vanilla. Add the flour mixed with baking powder, soda and salt. Mix well and spoon the dough into balls about 1 inch in diameter. Place these on an oiled pan or the oiled bottom of the oven; flatten the dough balls with a floured fork. You may cook in multiple batches or use several ovens.

Bake about 15 minutes.

Makes about 40

BANANA LOAF

½ cup butter	½ tsp salt
½ cup brown sugar	1 tsp baking soda
2 eggs, beaten	2 cups mashed bananas
1 cup whole wheat flour	¼ cup milk
1 cup quick oats	

In a bowl, blend the butter and sugar; then add the beaten eggs. In another bowl, mix flour, oats, salt and soda; then add this to blended mixture. Add bananas and milk; then stir well. Pour batter into an oiled pan and bake it in the oven for about 50–60 minutes. Turn out of pan onto serving plate.

Serves 8

Variation

Add chopped pecans to batter, or place pecans in baking pan before pouring batter into the pan.

CHOCOLATE FOLLY

Crust:

1¾ cups graham crackers, crushed

½ cup butter, melted

1½ tbsp cocoa

4 tbsp sugar

Filling:

1 tbsp cocoa

½ cup flour

1 cup sugar

½ cup butter, melted

1 egg, beaten

½ tsp almond flavoring

Topping:

5 tbsp butter

6 oz semisweet chocolate

1 cup small marshmallows or ½ cup semisweet chocolate chips

Crust: Combine graham crackers, sugar and cocoa and mix well. Add the butter to the dry ingredients and stir until thoroughly mixed. Press the mixture firmly into the bottom and ½ inch up the side of an oiled 9-inch round pan.

Filling: Combine cocoa, flour and sugar in the bowl. Add the butter and stir. When the mixture is blended, add the egg and flavoring and stir well. Pour this filling into the crust and bake for 30 minutes. Remove from the oven and set aside.

Topping: Melt the butter and chocolate in a sauce pan on low heat. Place the marshmallows or the chocolate chips on top of the cooked filling, and pour the melted butter and chocolate sauce on top of the filling.

When the dish is cool, cut it into small wedge servings.

Serves 8

CHOCOLATE LAYER PUDDING

Lower layer:

¾ cup sugar

1½ cup flour

2 tbsp baking powder

¼ tsp salt

1 1-oz square of
   unsweetened chocolate

3 tbsp butter

1 cup milk

1 tsp almond flavoring

Upper layer:

1 cup brown sugar

2 tbsp cocoa

1 cup boiling water

Lower layer: Place sugar, flour, baking powder and salt in a mixing bowl, mix well and set aside. Melt chocolate and butter in a sauce pan; then stir in the milk and almond flavoring. Add this liquid to the sugar and flour mixture; mix well, and place this dough into an oiled baking pan.

Upper layer: Mix sugar and cocoa together and spread over the dough mixture in the baking pan. Pour 1 cup of boiling water on the top of this layer; place the pan in the oven and bake for 35 minutes. Remove the pan from the oven; serve the pudding warm.

Serves 6–8

FUDGE SQUARES

¾ cup butter

½ cup cocoa

¾ cup flour

1½ cups sugar

1 tsp vanilla

3 eggs, beaten

½ cup toasted chopped pecans

Heat butter and cocoa until butter melts; set aside. Mix flour and sugar in a bowl; add vanilla and the beaten eggs. Add butter and cocoa ingredients to the mixture; stir in pecans.

Pour batter into an oiled baking pan or directly into the oven. Cover and bake for 40–50 minutes. Remove cake to cool about 15 minutes and cut into squares.

Serves 8

BREAD PUDDING

½ cup butter	½ cup raisins
1½ cups milk	⅛ tsp salt
1 cup sugar	3 eggs
4 cups day-old bread, cubed	cinnamon

Melt butter in pan, add milk and heat until bubbles form at edge of pan. Add sugar and stir until sugar dissolves. Add bread cubes, raisins and salt. Beat eggs and stir into mixture. Pour into an oiled baking pan; then sprinkle cinnamon on top.

Place baking pan in oven and bake 40–50 minutes. When done, serve on plates and add dessert sauce (recipe follows), if desired.

Serves 8

Variations

1. Use brown sugar on top rather than cinnamon.
2. Use yogurt rather than a sauce.

DESSERT SAUCE

½ cup sugar	3 tbsp butter
1 tbsp cornstarch	2 tbsp lemon juice
1 cup water	

Combine sugar, cornstarch and water in pan. Stir mixture over low coals until thickened; remove from heat. Add butter and lemon juice, stirring until sauce is smooth. Pour sauce on dessert item.

Variations

1. Instead of lemon juice, use orange juice, cherry juice or a flavoring.
2. Add a few raisins to the sauce.

WONDER PUDDING

2 cups graham cracker crumbs

3 tbsp sugar

¾ cup butter

1 cup semisweet
  chocolate pieces

1 14-oz can sweetened
  condensed milk

Mix graham cracker crumbs, sugar and warmed butter; press on the bottom and sides of baking pan. Place chocolate pieces in pan; then pour milk on top.

Bake about 25 minutes, or until pudding is browning on edge. Cool and cut into small servings.

Serves 8

TRAIL CAKE

2 cups hot water

2 cups brown sugar

1 tbsp butter

½ cup raisins

1 tsp salt

1 tsp cinnamon

3 cups flour

1 tsp baking soda

In a pan, mix water, sugar, butter, raisins, salt and cinnamon. Bring to a boil and simmer for 5 minutes. Remove pan from fire and cool completely.

Combine flour and soda; add to cooled liquid; mix and place in an oiled baking pan. Cook for about 50 minutes.

Serves 8–10

Variation

Add ¼ cup chopped pecans to flour mixture.

MINCEMEAT LOAF

2 cups flour	2 eggs
1 cup sugar	¼ cup butter, melted
1 tbsp baking powder	1 tsp vanilla
½ tsp salt	9 oz mincemeat

Mix flour, sugar, baking powder and salt in a bowl. In separate bowl, beat eggs; add melted butter and vanilla; mix with dry ingredients. Stir in mincemeat, prepared as directed on package. Pour batter into an oiled baking pan.

Bake 1 hour or until batter is done through the center. Cool 15 minutes and remove from container.

Serves 8–10

Variations

1. Add ¼ cup chopped pecans to batter.

2. In a small bowl, mix 1 cup confectioners' sugar and 1 tbsp milk; stir to smooth glaze. Pour glaze on cake top.

3. Sprinkle confectioners' sugar on cake after it is removed from oven.

APPLESAUCE CAKE

1 cup butter	2 tsp baking soda
2 cups brown sugar	½ tsp salt
1 16-oz can applesauce	2 tsp cinnamon
3 cups flour	

Cream butter and sugar; mix in applesauce. Combine flour, soda, salt and cinnamon and stir into the mixture. Place in oiled baking pan and bake for 50–60 minutes.

Serves 8–10

Notes

Notes

BREADS

BISCUITS

biscuit mix   flour

Mix 12–18 oz of biscuit mix as directed and pat out to $\frac{1}{2}$-inch thickness on floured, flat surface. Cut biscuits with a small open-end can and place 20–24 biscuits in oven. Cover and bake about 15 minutes.

Instead of using a flat surface, you may use floured hands and roll dough into $1\frac{1}{2}$-inch balls. Then flatten into biscuit shape and place in oven.

For drop biscuits, the mixed dough can be spooned into the oven without any shaping.

Makes about 20

FARM BISCUITS

3 cups flour   6 tbsp cooking oil
6 tsp baking powder   1 cup milk
$\frac{1}{2}$ tsp salt

Mix all ingredients. Roll on flat, floured surface to $\frac{1}{2}$-inch thickness; cut biscuits with a thin cutter and place in bottom of oven. Cover with lid and bake about 15 minutes.

Makes about 20

PLANTATION PONE BREAD

2 cups cornmeal   1½ cups boiling water
1 tsp salt   cooking oil
3 tbsp butter

Mix cornmeal, salt and butter. Add the boiling water (water must be boiling). Stir the ingredients; wet your hands and shape mixture into pones or patties about biscuit size and ½-inch thick.

Fry in cooking oil until golden, turning once; remove and drain. Serve hot.

Serves 8

SOUTHERN CORN BREAD

2 cups cornmeal   1¼ cups milk
1 tbsp baking powder   2 eggs
½ tsp salt   2 tbsp cooking oil
4 tbsp flour

Mix the cornmeal, baking powder, salt and flour; then add milk and mix. Add eggs and oil; stir. Pour into greased muffin pan or cupcake holders or onto bottom of hot oven. Bake 20–25 minutes in covered oven.

Serves 8

Variations

1. Spanish Corn Bread: *Add pieces of chopped pimento or bell pepper to mix.*
2. Herbed Corn Bread: *Add 1 tbsp of dill weed or parsley flakes to the cornmeal.*

DUMPLINGS

biscuit mix   flour

Prepare biscuit dough mixture either from a dry biscuit mix or from basic ingredients. Roll on floured surface or pat by hand and form biscuits of 1- to 1½-inch diameter. Place these biscuits on top of contents of oven, cover and cook about 30 minutes. You may want to spoon the dough into small balls and drop them into the stewing food.

BASIC BANNOCK BREAD

1 cup flour   ½ tsp salt
1 tbsp baking powder   water

Mix ingredients with a few tablespoons of water. Place in hot oven, cover and bake 20–30 minutes. The dough can bake as one large loaf or several small ones.

Serves 3–4

Variations
  1. Milk instead of water adds flavor and makes a browner loaf.
  2. One to two tbsp sugar adds flavor and crispness.
  3. One egg makes bread richer.
  4. One to two tbsp cooking oil makes bread flakier.
  5. Add cinnamon or flavorings as desired.

OVEN TOAST

butter   bread

Melt butter in open oven. Place pieces of bread on bottom of oven, turning when brown on one side. Continue adding butter as more bread is toasted.

FRENCH TOAST BATTER

8 eggs	bread
2 cups milk	butter
½ tsp salt	syrup, jelly or powdered sugar

Place eggs, milk and salt in bowl and mix thoroughly. Place 2 tbsp butter on inverted lid or on bottom of open oven. Dip slices of bread in the batter mix and then brown in open oven or on lid. Turn once and brown on other side. Continue adding butter as needed.

Serve hot with warm syrup, jelly or powdered sugar.

Variation

Add cinnamon to batter.

MUFFINS

1¾ cups flour	1 egg, beaten
3 tbsp sugar	1 cup milk
1 tbsp baking powder	6 tbsp cooking oil
¾ tsp salt	

Place flour, sugar, baking powder and salt in a bowl. Add egg, milk and cooking oil to the bowl and stir until the batter is smooth.

Place cupcake papers in a muffin pan or cupcake holders. If cupcake papers are not used, place 1 tsp of cooking oil into each muffin cup holder.

Fill cupcake papers or muffin cups about ²/₃ full of batter. Bake 20–25 minutes in covered oven.

Serves 8

Variations

1. Add ¹/₂ cup raisins or fresh fruit to batter.
2. Add cinnamon or nutmeg to batter.
3. Add vanilla, almond or lemon flavoring.

HOMESTEAD PANCAKES

2½ cups flour	2 eggs, beaten
2 tbsp baking powder	1½ cups milk
2 tbsp sugar	4 tbsp butter or cooking oil
½ tsp salt	maple syrup

Mix ingredients well. Cook batter in 3-inch diameter cakes on inverted, heated, oiled lid of oven. Three or four cakes can be cooked at the same time.

Serve with butter and warm maple syrup.

Makes about 30

LOAF BREAD

1 pkg dry yeast	1 tsp salt
¼ cup warm water (not hot)	1 tbsp sugar
1 cup warm milk (not hot)	3 cups flour
1 tbsp butter	

Mix dry yeast in water; stir to dissolve. Add milk, butter, salt and sugar; stir well. Add flour in small amounts (retaining ½ cup) and mix thoroughly. The dough will be stiff. Sprinkle some of the remaining flour on a flat surface. Knead dough by folding in into the middle from the outside and mashing it down in the middle. Knead until dough is smooth.

Place dough in greased bowl; cover bowl and set in a warm place until dough doubles, about 1 hour.

Punch dough down, folding and mashing out air pockets. Shape dough into a smooth oval roll and place in greased baking pan. Cover pan and keep in a warm place until dough doubles, about 30–40 minutes.

Bake in a covered oven 30–40 minutes or until top of loaf is golden brown. When done, remove pan from oven and set pan aside for 5 minutes. Then remove bread from pan.

Serves 8

Variations

1. *On last kneading, fold in cinnamon, brown sugar and raisins to make raisin bread.*
2. *Substitute a cup of onion soup for the milk; add 2 tsp minced onion for onion bread.*
3. *Add ¹/₄ tsp garlic salt to dough for garlic bread.*

HUDSON BAY BREAD

2 cups butter	10 cups rolled oats, finely chopped
2 cups sugar	
⅓ cup light corn syrup	1 cup almonds, finely chopped
⅓ cup honey	

Blend butter, sugar, syrup and honey. Add oats and almonds and mix well. A few tablespoons of flour added at this point will give additional smoothness to the bread texture.

Place batter into a greased baking pan in the oven; cover with the lid and bake about 20 minutes.

Remove the pan from the oven and allow it to cool. The bread may be sliced later for serving.

Serves 8

CHEESE BREAD

4 cups flour	1⅓ cups milk
4 tbsp sugar	⅓ lb cheese, grated
½ tsp salt	1 cup butter
1 pkg yeast	

Mix 1 cup flour, sugar, salt and yeast in a bowl. Add warmed milk and mix thoroughly. Add cheese and butter; mix. Add remaining flour; mix well and set aside in a warm place. Allow dough to double, about 1 hour.

Punch dough down; wait 15 minutes. Punch dough down again; form into round ball in a pan and allow dough to double, about 1 hour. Place in covered oven and bake about 30 minutes or until golden brown.

Serves 8

ONE-LOAF BREAD

1¼ cups warm water

1 pkg dry yeast

2 tbsp cooking oil

½ tsp salt

2 tbsp sugar

1½ cups whole wheat flour

1½ cups white flour

Dissolve yeast in water. Add oil, salt, sugar and half of the flours. Stir until mixed; gradually add the remaining flours and stir until smooth.

Put the dough into an oiled pan, cover and place the pan in a contained space to allow the dough to rise undisturbed for about 60 minutes. This space can be a cabinet, a cold oven, or even a corrugated cardboard box.

With floured hands, knead the dough well and shape into a roll, placing the roll in an oiled loaf pan. Let the dough rise until about double the size of the original and bake 35–40 minutes in oven.

Remove pan from the oven and let it cool for a few minutes. Shake pan to loosen the bread and remove it from the pan. Place loaf of bread on a cooling rack until it is cool enough to slice.

Makes one loaf

Notes

Notes

⌐ SOURDOUGH ⌐

SOURDOUGH STARTER WITH YEAST

1 envelope yeast	1 tbsp sugar
1½ cups warm water (not hot)	1 tsp salt
2 cups flour	

Dissolve yeast in warm water; then mix in other ingredients. Place the dough into a covered dish and set aside in a warm place for 1 or 2 days.

Always leave at least 1 cup of starter for seed. Replenish with 1 cup flour and 1 cup milk or water. Starter action may be delayed for several days by storage in refrigeration.

SOURDOUGH STARTER WITHOUT YEAST

2 cups flour	2 tbsp sugar
½ tsp salt	2 cups warm water

Mix well and store in a covered dish for several days in a warm place.

Always leave at least 1 cup of starter for seed. Replenish with 1 cup flour and 1 cup milk or water. Starter action may be delayed for several days by storage in refrigeration.

MINERS' MUFFINS

1 cup sourdough starter	1 egg
2 cups flour	2 tbsp cooking oil
½ cup milk	1 tsp baking powder
½ cup sugar	½ tsp salt

Mix all ingredients and cook in muffin pans or cupcake holders for about 30 minutes in covered oven.

You may want to add a few drops of cooking oil to the bottom of each cupcake paper to aid in keeping this dough from sticking to the paper.

Makes 12–15

Variations

1. Add raisins or berries.
2. Add lemon, almond or vanilla flavoring.

'49ER PANCAKES

½ cup sourdough starter	1 tbsp sugar
2 cups flour	1 tbsp cooking oil
1 cup milk	1 tbsp baking powder
2 eggs	butter
½ tsp salt	maple syrup

Mix all ingredients well. Cook on inverted, heated, oiled lid of oven. Serve with butter and warm maple syrup.

Makes about 25

WESTERN BISCUITS

1 cup sourdough starter	½ cup butter
2 cups flour	2 tsp baking powder
⅓ cup milk	½ tsp salt

Mix all ingredients; pat out on flat, floured surface to about ½-inch thickness. Cut out biscuits with a thin cutter and place in oven. Cook until golden brown.

Makes about 25

RANCHERS' BREAD

1 envelope yeast

1½ cups warm water (not hot)

1 cup sourdough starter

⅓ cup sugar

5 cups flour

3 tbsp cooking oil

2 tsp salt

Dissolve yeast in warm water; mix with other ingredients. Set to rise in oiled or floured container until double in volume, about 1–2 hours. Punch down and divide into number of loaves desired; put into greased pan(s) or on bottom of oven. Allow loaves to rise 1 hour. Bake about 30–40 minutes in covered oven.

Serves 8–12

MOUNTAIN COBBLER

1 cup sourdough starter

1½ cups flour

½ cup brown sugar

½ cup sugar

2 tsp cinnamon

½ cup cooking oil

2 cans cherry pie filling

Mix starter, flour, sugars, cinnamon and oil in a bowl. Place cherry filling in bottom of oven; then spread the bowl of mix on top. Bake 25–30 minutes in covered oven.

Serves 8

Variations

1. Use blueberry filling instead of cherry filling.

2. Add 1 cup of raisins with the fruit filling.

3. Add ¹/₂ cup of chopped pecans.

Notes

Notes

APPENDIX

*T*o provide assistance in your use of Dutch ovens, you may want to consider these items for your cooking equipment:

- Lid lifter with two support hooks allows lifting the coal-laden lid to inspect or serve food and prevents ashes from spilling into food.
- Small shovel moves coals from the fire. Coals can then be placed under and on the oven, as needed.
- Container of vegetable shortening.
- Gloves with leather palms.
- Padded pot holders.
- Soft mesh pot scrubber.
- Cotton terry-cloth wiping cloth pieces, about 6 inches square.
- Hot pot tongs.

INDEX